Black Family Research

Records of Post-Civil War Federal Agencies at the National Archives

■ ■ ■ ■ ■ ■

Compiled by Reginald Washington

Reference Information Paper 108

NATIONAL ARCHIVES AND RECORDS ADMINISTRATION
WASHINGTON, DC
REVISED 2010

United States. National Archives and Records Administration.
   Black family research: records of post-Civil War Federal agencies at the National Archives/compiled by Reginald Washington—Washington, DC: National Archives and Records Administration, revised 2010.
   ___ p.; 23 cm.—(Reference Information Paper 108)

   1. United States. Bureau of Refugees, Freedmen, and Abandoned Lands—History—Sources—Bibliography—Catalogs. 2. United States. Commissioners of Claims—History—Sources—Bibliography—Catalogs. 3. United States. Freedman's Bank and Trust Company—History—Sources—Bibliography—Catalogs. 4. Afro-Americans—United States—Genealogy. 5. Freedmen—History—Archival resources. 6. Registers of births, etc.—United States. I. Washington, Reginald. II. Title.

Front cover: *"Gwine to da Field." Freedmen who entered Union lines during the Civil War were often put to work on lands under Federal Government control. Freedmen shown here worked on the James Hopkinson plantation at Edisto Island, South Carolina. (64-CN-8971)*

Back cover: *The Freedmen's Bureau was responsible for issuing rations and clothing to destitute freedmen and refugees. This policy originated with the U.S. Army, which provided relief to needy slaves who fled into Union lines. (111-BA-2212)*

Introduction

The National Archives and Records Administration (NARA) is the official repository of the permanently valuable records of the U.S. Government. NARA's vast holdings document the lives and experiences of persons who interacted with the Federal Government. The records created by post–Civil War Federal agencies are perhaps some of the most important records available for the study of black family life and genealogy. Reconstruction-era Federal records document the black family's struggle for freedom and equality and provide insight into the Federal Government's policies toward the nearly 4 million African Americans freed at the close of the American Civil War. The records are an extremely rich source of documentation for the African American family historian seeking to "bridge the gap" for the transitional period from slavery to freedom.

This reference information paper describes three post–Civil War Federal agencies' records housed at NARA in Washington, DC, and College Park, MD: the Bureau of Refugees, Freedmen, and Abandoned Lands; the Freedman's Savings and Trust Company; and the Commissioners of Claims. Records of these agencies often provide considerable personal data about the African American family and community, including family relations, marriages, births, deaths, occupations, and places of residence. They can contain the names of slave owners and information concerning black military service, plantation conditions, manumissions, property ownership, migration, and a host of family related matters. While these records represent a major source for African American genealogical research at NARA, there are other Federal records available to assist the black family researcher as well. For details of these records, researchers should consult the *Guide to Genealogical Research in the National Archives* (National Archives Trust Fund Board, 2000); *Black Studies: A Select Catalog of National Archives Microfilm Publications* (National Archives Trust Fund Board, 2007); and *Black History: A Guide to Civilian Records in the National Archives* (General Services Administration, 1981).

Records of the Bureau of Refugees, Freedmen, and Abandoned Lands

The Bureau of Refugees, Freedmen, and Abandoned Lands (**Record Group [RG] 105**), also known as the Freedmen's Bureau, was established in the War Department by an act of Congress on March 3, 1865. The Bureau was responsible for the supervision and management of all matters relating to the refugees and freedmen and lands abandoned or seized during the Civil War, duties previously shared by military commanders and U.S. Treasury Department officials. In May 1865, President Andrew Johnson appointed Maj. Gen. Oliver Otis Howard as Commissioner of the Freedmen's Bureau. Howard's headquarters were in Washington, DC, but assistant commissioners, subassistant commissioners, and agents conducted the Bureau's daily operations in the former Confederate states, the border states, and the District of Columbia.

Although the Bureau was not abolished until 1872, the bulk of its work was conducted from June 1865 to December 1868. While a major part of the Bureau's early activities included the supervision of aban-

Most Freedmen came in contact with the Freedmen's Bureau at the local level such as at this office in Beaufort, South Carolina. (165-C-394)

doned and confiscated property, its mission was to provide relief and help freedmen become self-sufficient. Bureau functions included issuing rations and clothing, operating hospitals and refugee camps, and supervising labor contracts between planters and freedmen. The Bureau also managed apprenticeship disputes and complaints, assisted benevolent societies in the establishment of schools, helped freedmen in legalizing marriages entered into during slavery, and provided transportation to refugees and freedmen who were attempting to reunite with their family or relocate to other parts of the country.

As Congress extended the life of the Bureau, it added other duties, such as assisting black soldiers and sailors in obtaining back pay, bounty payments, and pensions. When the Bureau was discontinued, its remaining functions were transferred to the Freedmen's Branch of the Adjutant General's Office. The records of this office are among the Bureau's files. *Records of the Field Offices of the Freedmen's Branch, Office of the Adjutant General, 1872–1878* **(NARA Microfilm M2029, 58 rolls)** contains extensive genealogical information concerning black soldiers' and sailors' claims for bounty, pension, arrears of pay, commutation of rations, and prize money. The records can be valuable when used in conjunction with military service and pension records.

Because the Bureau's records contain a wide range of data about the African American experience during slavery and freedom, they are an invaluable source for the black family historian. Among the records are registers that give the names, ages, and former occupations of freedmen and names and residences of former owners. In addition, there are marriage registers that provide the names, addresses, ages, and complexions of husbands and wives and their children. For some states there are census lists, details of labor and apprenticeship agreements, complaint registers, personal data about black soldiers (including company and regiment), and a variety of documentation relating to the social and economic conditions of the black family.

Headquarters Records

Records of the Freedmen's Bureau, Washington, DC, headquarters consist of records of Commissioner Oliver Otis Howard and his staff. They have been described in *Records of the Bureau of Refugees Freedmen, and Abandoned Lands, Washington Headquarters* (**Preliminary Inventory 174**). The inventory descriptions of the Washington office are arranged by offices or divisions. Generally, researchers are less likely to find family related information among headquarter's files; however, because assistant commissioners and their subordinates forwarded a variety of reports and other documents to the Washington headquarters, the records can contain genealogical information.

For example, a series of marriage records among the headquarters' files includes freedmen's marriage certificates, licenses, reports, and other documents relating to marriages, covering the period 1861–69, with most dated between 1865 and 1868. It appears that this series was compiled or brought together by the Adjutant General's Office after the Freedmen's Bureau was abolished. These records for Alabama, Arkansas, Delaware, Florida, Kentucky, Louisiana, Mississippi, Missouri, Tennessee, South Carolina, Virginia, and the District of Columbia have been reproduced on microfilm (**NARA Microfilm M1875, 5 rolls**). However, the number and the type of records found vary for each state. The files for Louisiana, Mississippi, and Tennessee contain the greatest number of marriage certificates. These various marriage records can provide dates and places of marriages, and the names of couples, parents, former spouses, children, and the individual who performed the marriage ceremony.

In a letter to the Washington headquarters, Robert K. Scott, assistant commissioner for the State of South Carolina, included lists of destitute people in South Carolina. The lists are arranged alphabetically by county or city. They provide the name, sex, age, race, number of family members, the amount of land the person had to seed, and general remarks about the physical and economic condition of each destitute person.

Field Office Records

Records of the Bureau's field offices consist of records received and created by the assistant commissioners of the states and their subordinate officers. While the organizational structure under each assistant commissioner varied from state to state, subordinate officials in each state performed similar work. Field offices were inconsistent however, in the kinds of records they created. Thus, certain kinds of series available for some states may not exist for others. It is important to note that most people came in contact with the Bureau at the local level. Therefore, the vast majority of series that contain genealogical data can be found among these files.

For instance, there is an estimated 60 linear feet or more of labor contracts between blacks and planters among the field office records. Most contracts are from the Deep South and some include agreements with entire families. In the records of the assistant commissioner for Mississippi there are four marriage registers and nine such registers in various field offices in Arkansas. There are also marriage records for the assistant commissioners for the District of Columbia and marriage registers, lists, certificates, and licenses for several field offices in Kentucky. At least six field offices for Virginia contain census returns and lists. The records of the assistant commissioner for the District of Columbia, whose jurisdiction included parts of Maryland and Virginia, have census returns for the District, and in Virginia for Alexandria, Freedmen's Village, and Loudoun and Fairfax counties.

Other field office records of genealogical value are claims relating to the back pay, bounty payments, and pensions of black soldiers and sailors. There are claims registers and related records for every state, except Texas. These records can be used to supplement information found in the tens of thousands of military service and pension records of African American soldiers and sailors who served during the Civil War, particularly those who died in combat. Researchers should also examine files of letters sent and received by field officers. While these records often relate to Bureau operations, they do contain letters from and about African Americans and their families.

Intermixed with field office files are "pre-bureau" records that document the interactions of military commanders and U.S. Treasury agents with blacks during the Civil War. These records consist largely of files created by wartime superintendents of freedmen appointed by the War Department to manage "contraband" camps that provided food, clothing, and shelter to blacks entering Union lines. The most voluminous records are for Louisiana and Mississippi **(NARA Microfilm M1914, 5 rolls, and M1907, 65 rolls)** and fewer for Alabama, Arkansas, North Carolina, Tennessee, South Carolina, Virginia, and the District of Columbia. Many of the records contain registers that include the names and ages of blacks employed at the camps, addresses of former owners, lists of persons receiving rations, and information relating to the administration of abandoned and confiscated property. Other records relating to the activities of military commanders in areas where the Freedmen's Bureau operated can be found in the Records of the U.S. Army Continental Commands, 1821–1920 (RG 393). Records concerning the activities of

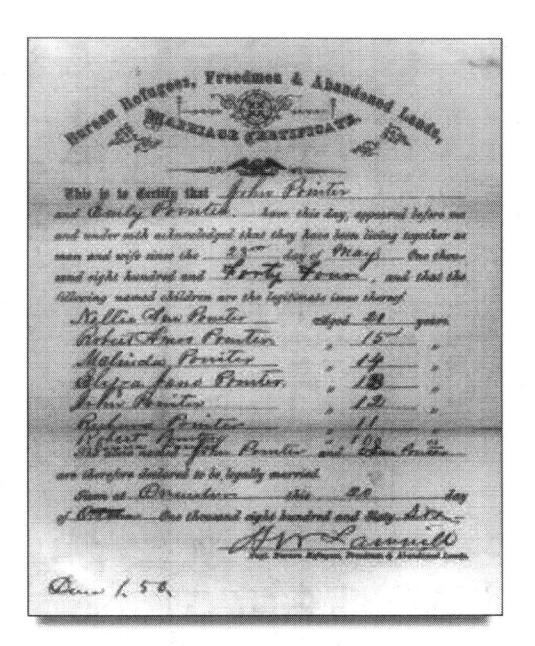

In 1866, Freedmen's Bureau officials at Owensboro, Kentucky, issued a marriage certificate to John and Emily Pointer that included the names and ages of their eight children. They had lived together as man and wife since 1844.

special agents of the Treasury Department are in the Records of Civil War Agencies of the Treasury Department (RG 366).

The surviving records of the Freedmen's Bureau field offices have been described in a three-part unpublished inventory entitled *Preliminary Inventory of the Records of the Field Offices of the Bureau of Refugees, Freedmen, and Abandoned Lands* (NM 95). The inventory descriptions of the records are arranged alphabetically by state and thereunder by offices, and thereunder alphabetically by county, town, or village. Part One describes the records of the bureau offices in Alabama, Arkansas (including the Indian Territory), the District of Columbia, Florida, Georgia, Kentucky, and Louisiana. Part Two includes descriptions for offices in Maryland and Delaware, Mississippi, Missouri, North Carolina, and South Carolina. Part Three covers offices in Tennessee, Texas, Virginia, and the records of the Freedmen's branch of the Adjutant General's Office. In addition to providing the locations of the headquarters of state assistant commissioners and subordinate offices, the inventory gives the names and dates of service of individual officers. This information can be helpful in identifying Bureau officials who might have sent and received correspondence on behalf of or about blacks and their families.

Access and Use of the Records

The original Freedmen's Bureau records are available at the National Archives Building in Washington, DC. For access and inquiries about the use of the records, researchers should visit or write the Archives I Reference Section (NWCT1R). Selected records of the Bureau's Washington headquarters and all field offices have been reproduced on microfilm. Most of the field records that were microfilmed prior to 2002 relate to the administrative files of the state assistant commissioners and superintendents of education. The exception is the series of field office records for New Orleans (**NARA Microfilm M1483, 10 rolls**), which contains such records as labor contracts, hospital registers, complaint books, and indentures of apprentices. The records of the field offices for Florida (**NARA Microfilm M1869, 15 rolls**) have been microfilmed through a cooperative arrangement between NARA and the University of Florida at Gainesville. With the support of Congress, the National Archives completed a multiyear project to preserve and increase the accessibility of field office records, especially those of the subordinate field offices, where researchers are more likely to find records of genealogical value. NARA has microfilmed the field office records for Alabama (**NARA Microfilm M1900, 34 rolls**), Arkansas (**NARA Microfilm M1901, 23 rolls**), the District of Columbia (**NARA Microfilm M1902, 21 rolls**), Georgia (**NARA Microfilm M1903, 90 rolls**), Kentucky (**NARA Microfilm M1904, 133 rolls**), Louisiana

(**NARA Microfilm M1905, 111 rolls**), Maryland/ Delaware (**NARA Microfilm M1906, 42 rolls**), Mississippi (**NARA Microfilm M1907, 65 rolls**), Missouri (**NARA Microfilm M1908, 24 rolls**), North Carolina (**NARA Microfilm M1909, 78 rolls**), South Carolina (**NARA Microfilm M1910, 106 rolls**), Tennessee (**NARA Microfilm M1911, 89 rolls**), Texas (**NARA Microfilm M1912, 28 rolls**), and Virginia (**NARA Microfilm M1913, 203 rolls**). All of the field office records are available on microfilm at the National Archives Building, Washington, DC, and at each of NARA's regional facilities. For a list of some of NARA's Freedmen's Bureau microfilm publications and their content, researchers should consult the current edition of the *Black Studies* microfilm catalog. This guide is available for sale at *www.estore.archives.gov* or at the Customer Service Center in Washington, DC, or can be ordered from the Research Support Branch (NWCC2). Most Freedmen's Bureau microfilm publications have accompanying descriptive pamphlets (DPs) that include a brief history of the Bureau, a description of the records, and an explanation of the arrangement of the records. DPs can be viewed online or obtained free of cost through the Research Support Branch (NWCC1). Copies of some of the previously filmed publications may be available at NARA's regional records services centers. For information on availability, researchers should contact the nearest regional center or visit NARA's Order Online web page at *www.archives.gov*.

Copies of inventories for both the Washington headquarters of the Bureau and field office records are available at the National Archives Building in Washington, DC, and at NARA's regional records services facilities. While the inventories for the Washington headquarters and the *Black Studies* guide should be examined for record series of potential genealogical value, researchers should first consult the preliminary inventories of field office records for the geographic location in which an ancestor resided. If there are no records available for the state, city, or county in which an ancestor lived, family historians will need to examine the inventories and records for neighboring states, counties, and cities. Researchers should identify and search series in field office records that are likely to contain genealogical information (e.g., labor contracts, ration lists and applications, census lists, contracts of indentures, complaint records, marriage records, military claims, etc.) Because of their potential for containing information from and about African Americans, researchers should also search letters sent and received by Bureau officials.

Researchers interested in using Freedmen's Bureau records should bear in mind that they are voluminous and, at times, difficult to use. The headquarter's records and those for the field offices of the state assistant and subordinate offices consist of more than 1,000 cubic feet of records and contain nearly 5,000 separate series. While the records are a treasure trove of information for the study of the black family experience before and after the Civil War, they lack useful name indexes, and, in some instances, the arrangement of the records prevents easy access. Thus, research in the records can be time consuming when looking for individuals. Below are general descriptions of some of the most common record series and those that are apt to include genealogical data:

- **Labor contracts:** Contracts between freedmen and employers (usually farmers or plantation owners) witnessed by Bureau officers. Most of the contracts provide the names of the contracting parties, the period of service, the rate of wages, and type of work to be performed.
- **Registers of labor contracts:** Registers kept by officers subordinate to assistant commissioners. The registers usually give the date of the contract, the names of the contracting parties, and the rate of wages.
- **Registers and applications of persons receiving rations:** The registers and applications can include the name of the head of family, names of the wife and children, ages of children, location of land, number of cultivated acres, owner of land, and the date that rations were issued.
- **Indentures:** Indentures of apprenticeship are preprinted or handwritten forms giving pertinent data concerning the contracted parties and dates of apprenticeship, and include a statement of the obligations and responsibilities of each party. Registers of indentures provide the date, name of the person indentured, name of the officer who officiated, and name of the custodian to whom the person was indentured.
- **Registers of complaints:** Registers kept by officers subordinate to the assistant commissioners. The "complaints" relate to problems that freedmen brought to the officer's attention. Many of the registers simply list the name or names of the freedmen and the nature of the complaint, but others also give a synopsis or summary of the case.
- **Registers of marriages:** Registers kept by officers subordinate to the assistant commissioners. Most registers give the names of the couple, the date the marriage was registered, and the minister who performed the ceremony. Many registers also provide information about previous marriages and the number of children from these marriages.
- **Census lists:** Census lists can include the individual's name, age, sex, and residence; the name of former owner, if applicable, and the person's occupation and current employment.

- **Registers of claimants:** The registers were compiled by the disbursing officers and usually give the name of the claimant, his company and regiment, and the date he received money from the chief disbursing officer. Registers often contain the amount due the claimant, the date and place the claim was paid, and the person who identified the claimant.
- **List of claimants:** Each "List" was received from a disbursing officer. It is usually a printed form giving the name of the soldier or his heirs, and his rank, company, and regiment. Also provided is the name and residence of the agent, the number and amount of the Treasury certificate, the fees due the agent, and the amount paid to the claimant.
- **Letters sent:** Volumes containing copies of outgoing communications that usually include letters, telegrams, and reports made to superior officers.
- **Registers of letters received:** Volumes in which incoming communications were entered. Registers usually include the date received, the date written, the name and office of the writer, the place from which the letter was written, a summary of the contents, and the entry number assigned to the letter.
- **Letters received:** Incoming communications, usually consisting only of letters, but sometimes including reports and orders.

Internet Sources

Records of the Bureau of Refugees, Freedmen, and Abandoned Lands (Freedmen's Bureau)

Archives.gov
For additional information about Freedmen's Bureau records and links to other resources, visit the National Archives Freedmen's Bureau web page at http://www.archives.gov/research/african-americans/freedmens-bureau/

Ancestry.com
Ancestry has an online database *(http://search.ancestryinstitution.com/search/db.aspx?dbid+1105&enc+1)* of selected Freedmen's Bureau Assistant Commissioner and Field Office records. The database provides digital images of records reproduced on National Archives microfilm publications for the District of Columbia (**M1902, 21 rolls**), Georgia (**M1903, 90 rolls**), North Carolina (**M1909, 78 rolls**), New Orleans, Louisiana (**M1483, 10 rolls**), Florida (**M1869, Assistant Commissioner and Subordinated Field Offices, 15 rolls**), Virginia (**M1913, 203 rolls**), and Tennessee (**T142, 73 rolls**). The database is searchable by state, start and end year, type of record, and keyword(s).

Records of the Freedman's Savings and Trust Company

Incorporated by Congress by an act of March 3, 1865, the Freedman's Savings and Trust Company (also known as Freedman's Bank) was established as a banking institution primarily for the benefit of former slaves. Shortly after its creation, two military savings banks at Norfolk, VA, and Beaufort, SC, established during the Civil War for savings deposits of African American soldiers, were transferred to the company. Between 1865 and 1870 the Freedman's Bank opened some 37 branches in 17 states and the District of Columbia. Over its 9-year history, the bank had more than 70,000 depositors and deposits totaling more than $57 million.

In mid-1874, overwhelmed by the effects of the Panic of 1873, mismanagement, abuse, and fraud, the Freedman's Bank closed. By an act of June 20, 1874, the trustees, with the approval of the Secretary of the Treasury, appointed a three-member board to take charge of the assets of the company and report its financial condition to the Secretary of the Treasury. A later act of February 21, 1881, abolished the board and directed the Secretary of the Treasury to appoint the Comptroller of the Currency to oversee the affairs of the Bank. The Comptroller was made Commissioner *ex officio* and was required to submit annual reports to Congress. The Commissioner's final report on the Freedman's Bank was made in 1920.

Contrary to what many of its depositors were led to believe, the Bank's assets were not protected by the Federal Government. While half of the depositors eventually received about three-fifths of the value of their accounts, others received nothing. Well into the 20th century, some depositors and their heirs were still seeking reimbursement for the remaining portions of their accounts.

Registers of Signatures of Depositors

Required by law to protect the interests of the heirs of the depositors, the Bank branches collected an enormous amount of personal information about each depositor and his or her family. While the amount of information collected varied from branch to branch, the surviving records of registers of signatures of depositors are probably one of the few bodies of Federal records that provide so much detailed information about black family relations immediately following the Civil War.

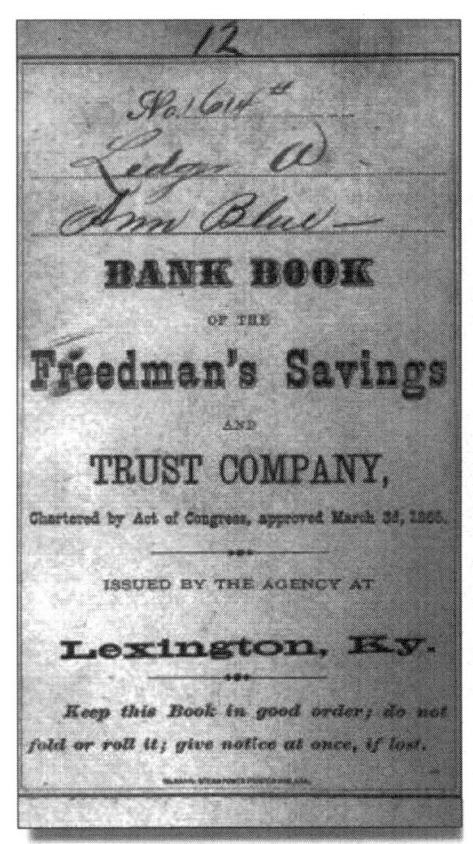

Former slaves who opened accounts with the Freedman's Bank were issued passbooks as evidence of their deposits. Ann Blue opened her account in the Lexington, Kentucky, branch office in August 1873.

Registers of Signatures of Depositors in Branches of the Freedman's Savings and Trust Company, 1865–1874 **(NARA Microfilm M816, 27 rolls)** reproduces 55 volumes containing signatures of and personal identification data about depositors in 29 branches of the Freedman's Bank. In addition to the name and account numbers of individual depositors, the files can contain information such as the age, complexion, place of birth, and place raised. The name of the former owner, mistress, and plantation appears in some of the earlier volumes. The files also include place of residence, occupation, parents, spouse, children, brothers and sisters, remarks, and signature. Some entries include death certificates.

The signatures of depositors are arranged alphabetically by state, thereunder by city in which the branch was located, then by date when the account was established, and finally by account number.

Indexes to Deposit Ledgers

The registers of signatures are not indexed. However, *Indexes to Deposit Ledgers in Branches of the Freedman's Savings and Trust Company, 1865–1874* **(NARA Microfilm M817, 5 rolls)** reproduces 46 volumes of indexes to deposit ledgers that provide the names of depositors in 26 branch offices of the Freedman's Bank. The indexes also provide account numbers of the deposit ledgers. Some volumes show the amount of the deposit. The deposit ledgers themselves are not in the National Archives, and it is not known if they still exist. The indexes are arranged alphabetically by state and thereunder by city in which the branch was located. The names are indexed, for the most part, alphabetically by the first letter of the surname. Because the index entries include account numbers, researchers can use them as a rough finding aid to the registers of signatures.

A note of caution, however, is advised when using the indexes. More than one index exists for some bank offices, and some indexes are not arranged in strict alphabetical order. In such cases, it is necessary to examine every name under the letter of the alphabet that begins the surname. In addition, some indexes do not list all depositors whose surnames appear in the registers of signatures; many account numbers are missing; and in some cases, account numbers assigned to depositors in the index are different from those in the signature cards. In this event, it is necessary to search entire rolls of signature cards for bank offices where an ancestor lived. If there were no bank offices in the state and city where an ancestor resided, researchers should search for information about ancestors in the records of branch offices in neighboring states and cities.

Below is a list of Freedman's Bank branch offices for which there are surviving signatures of depositors and indexes to deposit ledgers. Although there are indexes to deposit ledgers available for the Jacksonville, Florida, branch office, there are no surviving signature records. For a general listing

Bank Branches	Indexes	Bank Branches	Indexes
Huntsville, AL	Yes	Vicksburg, MS	Yes
Mobile, AL	No	St. Louis, MO	Yes
Little Rock, AR	Yes	New York, NY	Yes
Washington, DC	Yes	New Bern, NC	Yes
Tallahassee, FL	Yes	Raleigh, NC	Yes
Atlanta, GA	No	Wilmington, NC	Yes
Augusta, GA	Yes	Philadelphia, PA	Yes
Savannah, GA	Yes	Beaufort, SC	Yes
Lexington, KY	Yes	Charleston, SC	Yes
Louisville, KY	Yes	Memphis, TN	Yes
New Orleans, LA	Yes	Nashville, TN	Yes
Shreveport, LA	Yes	Lynchburg, VA	No
Baltimore, MD	Yes	Norfolk, VA	Yes
Columbus, MS	No	Richmond, VA	Yes
Natchez, MS	Yes		

Freedman's Bank officials sought deposits from African American soldiers like Paul Potter during the early years of the Bank expansion. His signature card is shown here.

of series contents for signature cards and indexes, researchers should examine the microfilm roll lists in either the *Black Studies* microfilm catalog or the Order Online locator at *www.archives.gov/order*.

Journal of the Board of Trustees and Minutes of Committees and Inspectors

A board of 50 trustees managed the Freedman's Bank. The *Journal of the*

Board of Trustees and Minutes of Committees and Inspectors of the Freedman's Savings and Trust Company, 1865–1874 (**NARA Microfilm M874, 2 rolls**) reproduces the *Journal of the Board of Trustees*; the minutes of the agency, finance, and building committees; and inspector's minutes. The journal and minutes are arranged chronologically by the date of the meeting. There are no minutes for the Educational and Improvement Committee, and those of the inspector are incomplete. While these records have little or no genealogical value, they can, however, be useful for studying the administrative activities and financial decisions of the company.

Other Records

Additional records concerning the Freedman's Bank and its failure are the loan and real estate ledgers and journals (1870–1916), and letters sent and received by the commissioners of the company and the Comptroller of the Currency as Commissioner *ex officio* (1874–1914). Also scattered among these records are legal papers, canceled checks, payrolls, expense checks, passbooks, and questionnaires. Correspondence, loan papers, and passbooks have been reproduced on microfilm by Lexis Nexis as the *Freedman's Savings and Trust Company: Letters Received by the Commissioners,* 1870–1914, Part 1: Correspondence, Loans and Bank Books **(Microfilm Publication C213).** The remaining records have yet to be microfilmed. While these records relate primarily to the liquidation of the Freedman's Bank, they can contain genealogical information, especially the questionnaires. Depositors and their heirs, who submitted claims for dividend payments, were required to send passbooks to Commissioners at Washington, DC. Those who were unable to supply passbooks had to complete a questionnaire that requested the same information supplied by depositors at the time they opened their accounts. These records are of particular importance when there are no signature records available to show that an individual had an account with the Freedman's Bank.

Related Records

Although established as a private corporation, the Freedman's Bank often shared offices rent-free with the Freedmen's Bureau. Many Freedmen's Bureau officials served as trustees and cashiers of the Freedman's Bank. John W. Alvord served as president of the Freedman's Bank (1868–74) while holding the position of general superintendent of education of the Freedmen's Bureau. The *Records of the Education Division of the Bureau of Refugees, Freedmen, and Abandoned Lands, 1865–1871* (**NARA Microfilm M803, roll 14**) are a series of registered letters received by Alvord in this dual role. Many of the letters relate to the activities of the Freedman's Bank.

Several committees of Congress investigated the Freedman's Bank closure and received petitions from persons who sought compensation for losses suffered when the Bank failed. Information concerning these matters can be found among the Records of the U.S. Senate (**RG 46**) and the U. S. House of Representatives (**RG 233**). For information concerning congressional holdings, researchers should visit or write to the Center for Legislative Archives. Researchers should also examine the Congressional Serial Set—a massive collection of publications of the U.S. Congress—for published reports and documents regarding the Freedman's Bank. The serial set is available at the National Archives and U.S. Government depository libraries throughout the country.

The signatures of depositors, indexes to deposit ledgers, the journal and minutes, and the Freedman's Bank records that have not been microfilmed, are a part of the Records of the Office of the Comptroller of the Currency (**RG 101**). Copies of microfilmed files are available at the National Archives facilities in Washington, DC, and in College Park, MD. Most of NARA's regional records services facilities also have copies of microfilmed records. Freedman's Bank records that have not been microfilmed are only available at the College Park facility. Written inquiries about the records should be referred to the National Archives Reference Sections listed in the appendix.

Internet Sources
Records of the Freedman's Savings and Trust Company (Freedman's Bank)

Heritage Quest
Heritage Quest has an online database *(http://persi.heritagequestionline.com/hqoweb/do/freedmans)* of persons who maintained accounts in the Freedman's Bank that is searchable by surname, given name, year, and bank location. The database provides digital images of records reproduced in *Registers of Signatures of Depositors in Branches of the Freedman's Savings and Trust Company,* 1865–1874 (**National Archives Microfilm Publication M816).**

Ancestry.com
Ancestry has a searchable online database to Freedman's Savings and Trust Company's registers of signatures of depositors *(http://search.ancestryinstitution.com/search/db.aspx?dbid=8755)*. The database provides digital images of records reproduced in *Registers of Signatures of Depositors in Branches of the Freedman's Savings and Trust Company,* 1865–1874 **(National Archives Microfilm Publication M816)**.

Records of the Commissioners of Claims

The Commissioners of Claims, commonly known as the Southern Claims Commission, was established by an act of Congress on March 3, 1871, to review and make recommendations regarding the claims of Southern Loyalists who had "furnished stores and supplies for the use of the U.S. Army" during the Civil War. Congress, by an act of May 11, 1872, extended this to include property taken or furnished to the U.S. Navy. Citizens who filed claims before the three-member board were required to show proof of loss of property and provide satisfactory evidence of their loyalty to the Federal Government throughout the war.

When the Commission ended on March 10, 1880, some 22,298 claims had been received. However, only 7,092 claims were approved. A small but impressive number of African Americans (former slaves and free blacks) filed claims, but the exact number is unknown. African Americans were also among the 222,000 witnesses who testified on behalf of African American and white claimants. Blacks who served as witnesses for other blacks were usually their relatives, fellow former slaves, or neighbors. African Americans who testified on behalf of whites were, in many instances, their former slaves.

The Commission's records contain an extraordinary amount of information useful for the study of Southern social history and the African American family including information concerning the names and ages of former slaves, their places of residence, and names of slave owners. The records also include information about plantation conditions, slaves as property owners, wills and probate matters, slave manumissions, slave and free black entrepreneurship, miscegenation, and other documentation about the lives and experiences of blacks during the slavery and the post-slavery periods.

Southern Claims Case Files

Southern claims files are found among the records of several Federal agencies at the National Archives. The allowed claims (claims approved in whole or in part) are among the settled accounts and claims of the Third Auditor of the Treasury in Records of the Accounting Officers of the Department of the Treasury (**Record Group [RG] 217**). The files are arranged by **state, thereunder by county, and then alphabetically by the claimant's name.** The approved case files for Alabama have been reproduced as

Southern Claims Commission Approved Claims, 1871–1880: Alabama (**NARA Microfilm M2062, 36 rolls**). The approved case files for Georgia have been reproduced as *Southern Claims Commission Approved Claims, 1871–1880: Georgia* (**NARA Microfiche M1658, 761 microfiche sheets**). The approved case files for West Virginia have been reproduced as *Southern Claims Commission Approved Claims, 1871–1880: West Virginia* (**NARA Microfilm M1762, 3 rolls**). The approved case files for Virginia have been reproduced as *Southern Claims Commission Approved Claims, 1871–1880: Virginia* (**NARA Microfilm M2094, 45 rolls**). Approved files for Arkansas, Florida, Louisiana, Mississippi, North Carolina, South Carolina, Tennessee, and Texas have not been microfilmed.

The disallowed case files and those that were barred, for failure to submit sufficient evidence by the deadline set by the Commission, are part of Records of the U.S. House of Representatives (**RG 233**). The disallowed files are arranged by **office and report number.** The approved and disallowed case files can contain similar types of documents such as claimant's petitions, depositions of neighbors and other persons, reports of the special agents, reports from the Treasury Department relative to its investigation of a claimant's disloyalty, and the final summary and recommendation of the commissioners. Because barred claims contain very little documentation, researchers will find them less informative for genealogical purposes. The files generally contain the original petition and little else. Any additional information found in the files usually concerns disloyalty. The barred

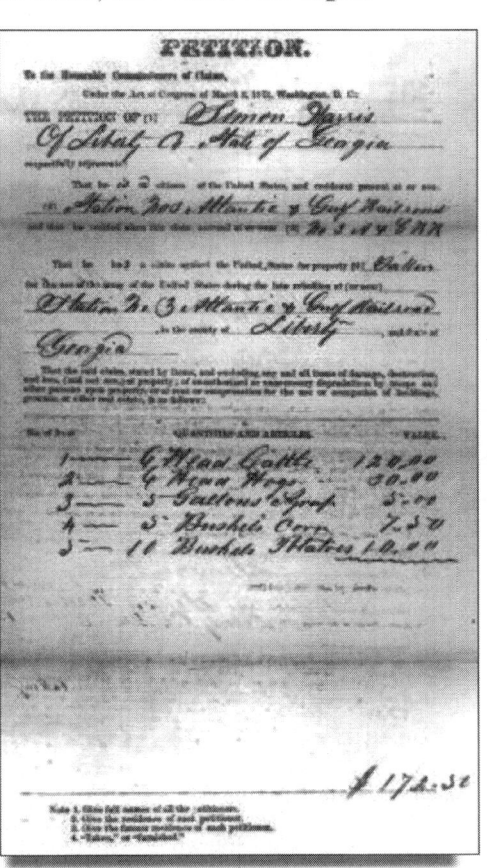

Simon Harris, a former slave from Liberty County, Georgia, provided the Southern Claims Commission with a petition listing personal property allegedly taken by the Union Army.

files are arranged alphabetically by **name of claimant**. Both the barred and disallowed files have been reproduced as *Barred and Disallowed Case Files of the Southern Claims Commission, 1871–1880* (**NARA Microfiche M1407, 4,829 microfiche sheets**).

Summary Reports

Congress published summaries of the disallowed claims in four volumes entitled *U.S. Commissioners of Claims Summary Reports in All Cases Reported to Congress as Disallowed Under the Act of March 3, 1871*. The African American family historian will find these volumes of particular importance. In each volume, African American claimants are identified as "former slaves," "colored," "free born," and "mulatto." In addition, the summaries provide an itemized list and the amount of compensation sought for goods furnished or seized by Federal troops. They also give a brief summary of evidence submitted regarding a claimant's ownership of property and loyalty; the state, county, and town where the claim was filed; the office and report number; the claim number; and the commissioners' reasons for disallowing the claim. The volumes have been reproduced on microfilm as *Records of the U.S. House of Representatives; A: Consolidated Index of Claims; B: Summary*

"Thinnin Corn." Slaves in some areas of the South were allowed to cultivate gardens set aside for them by their owners. From goods produced and sold from these tiny garden plots, slaves were able to accumulate property and, in some cases, purchase their freedom. (200s-HN-JOH (M)-24)

Reports of the Commissioners of Claims, 1871–1880 **(NARA Microfilm P2257, 1 roll**) and are available at the National Archives Building in Washington, DC, and many of the regional archives. Summary reports may be available at some NARA regional records services facilities and Government depository libraries.

U.S. Court of Claims

Under provisions of the Bowman Act of 1883 and the Tucker Act of 1887, any claims that had been previously barred or disallowed by the commission could be reconsidered by Congress and submitted to the U.S. Court of Claims for "findings of fact" but not a judgment. As a result, some of the original barred and disallowed Southern Claims are among the Records of the U.S. Court of Claims (**RG 123**). A notation in the file usually identifies claims that were sent to the Court. These files are accessed by court claims case file numbers, which have been reproduced as *U.S. Court of Claims Docket Cards for Congressional Case Files, ca. 1884–ca. 1943* (**NARA Microfilm M2007, 5 rolls**). Docket cards are arranged alphabetically by name of the claimant.

Other Records

Additional records relating to the Southern Claims Commission can be found in the General Records of the Department of the Treasury (**RG 56**). These records have been reproduced as *Records of the Commissioners of Claims (Southern Claims Commission), 1871–1880* (**NARA Microfilm M87, 14 rolls**). They include the journal of the Commissioners; miscellaneous letters received by the Commissioners; miscellaneous papers, consisting chiefly of memorandum copies of bills for goods; 57 summary reports; letters received by the commissioners from and about special agents; and a printed but unpublished geographical list of claims.

Searching a Claim

To determine whether an ancestor filed a claim before the Commission, researchers should first consult the *Consolidated Index of Claims Reported by the Commissioner of Claims to the House of Representatives, 1871–1880*. The index, for the most part, provides an alphabetical list of all persons who filed claims before the Commission (researchers should be aware of spelling variations when using the index). For the African American genealogist, however, the usefulness of this index is limited because it does not identify claimants by race. In addition, it is less helpful to those researchers interested in conducting research by individual counties. It does, nonetheless, include information necessary to locate an individual file, such as the state of residence; Commission number, office and report number; year of report; amount claimed; whether the claim was allowed, disallowed, barred, withdrawn, or dismissed; and the nature of the claim. The consolidated index has been reproduced on **NARA Microfilm M87, P2257,** and the first four microfiche of **M1407.**

Below are additional general procedures for researching Southern claims case files:

- For allowed claims not available on microfilm, researchers should contact the Archives II Reference Section (NWCT2R) at College Park, MD, to request a search for the files.
- For barred and disallowed claims, researchers should first consult **M1407** for the files. Written inquiries should be addressed to NARA's Center for Legislative Archives.
- For barred and disallowed claims that were forwarded to the U.S. Court of Claims, researchers should search **M2007** for the appropriate docket numbers. Once the docket numbers have been identified, researchers will need to contact the Archives I Reference Section (NWCT1R) in the National Archives Building in Washington, DC, to request a search for the records.
- For claims that were barred or disallowed that do not appear in U.S. Court of Claims files, researchers should contact the Center for Legislative Archives for a search among committee records of the U.S. House of Representatives for information relating to the records.
- Because former slaves frequently testified in the claims of persons who owned them, researchers should search the claims of individuals who filed claims from counties in which an ancestor resided.
- Researchers who want to do research by county or verify the county from which a claim was filed, should consult the geographical list of claims found on **M87** and *Southern Loyalists in the Civil War: The Southern Claims Commission* (Genealogical Publishing Co., Inc., 1994) by Gary B. Mills.

Internet Sources

Records of the Commissioners of Claims (Southern Claims Commission)

Ancestry.com
Ancestry has an online database of disallowed and barred claims *(http://search.ancestryinstitution.com/search/dv.aspx?dbid+1218)* searchable by first and last name; allowed claims *(http://search.ancestryinstitution.com/*

search/db.aspx?dbid=1217) for the states of Alabama, Georgia, Virginia, and West Virginia, are searchable by first and last name, state, and county. The database provides digital images of disallowed and barred claims reproduced in *Barred and Disallowed Case Files of the Southern Claims Commission,* 1871–1880 **(National Archives Microfilm Publication M1407 [4829 fiche])**; and digital images of records of allowed claims for the following states reproduced in microfilm publications **M2062** (Alabama, 36 rolls), **M1658** (Georgia, 761 microfiche sheets), **M2094** (Virginia, 45 rolls), and **M1762** (West Virginia, 3 rolls). The database also contains an index *(http://search.ancestryinstitution.com/search/db.aspx?dbid=1216)* to claims filed before the Southern Claims Commission.

Footnote.com

Footnote has an online database *(http://go.footnote.com/nara/)* of disallowed, barred, and allowed claims, searchable by first and last name, state, county, commission number, and date. The database provides digital images of disallowed and barred claims reproduced in **National Archives Microfilm Publication M1407**, and allowed claims reproduced on microfilm publications for the states of Alabama (**M2062**), Georgia (**M1658**), Virginia (**2094**), and West Virginia (**M1762**). Additional digital images of allowed claims reproduced from textual records (original records) for the states of Arkansas, Kentucky, North Carolina, and Tennessee are also searchable through the online database; other digital images of allowed claims for states of Florida, Louisiana, Mississippi, and South Carolina will be available for search once Footnote's digitization effort is completed.

NARA Offices to Contact

Freedmen's Bureau and U.S. Court of Claims Records
National Archives Building
Archives I Reference Section (NWCT1R)
700 Pennsylvania Avenue, NW
Washington, DC 20408-0001
archives1reference@nara.gov
Tel: 202-357-5363

Freedman's Bank Records
National Archives at College Park
Archives II Reference Section (NWCT2R)
8601 Adelphi Road
College Park, MD 20740-6001
archives2reference@nara.gov
Tel: 301-837-3510

Allowed Southern Claims Records
National Archives Building
Archives I Reference Section (NWCT1R)
700 Pennsylvania Avenue, NW
Washington, DC 20408-0001
archives1reference@nara.gov
Tel: 202-357-5363

Disallowed and Barred Southern Claims Records
National Archives and Records Administration
Center for Legislative Archives (NWL)
Room 205
700 Pennsylvania Avenue, NW
Washington, DC 20408-0001
Tel: 202-357-5350

To Contact NARA by E-mail

inquire@nara.gov

To Purchase NARA Publications

National Archives eStore
www.estore.archives.gov

or

Research Support Branch (NWCC2)
Room 1000
8601 Adelphi Road
College Park, MD 20740-6001
301-837-2000
1-866-272-6272
Fax 301-837-0483

To Research and Purchase Microfilm Publications

Visit Order Online at *www.archives.gov*

To Obtain Free NARA Publications

Research Support Branch (NWCC1)
Room G-13
700 Pennsylvania Avenue, NW
Washington, DC 20408-0001
202-357-5400
1-866-325-7208
Fax: 202-501-7170

Further Reading

Records of the Bureau of Refugees, Freedmen, and Abandoned Lands

George R. Bentley. *A History of the Freedmen's Bureau*. Philadelphia: Octagon Books, 1970.

Barry A. Crouch and Larry Madaras. "Reconstructing Black Families: Perspectives from the Texas Freedmen's Bureau Records." *Our Family, Our Town: Essays on Family and Local History Sources in the National Archives*. Washington, DC: National Archives and Records Administration, 1987, pp. 156–167.

Elaine C. Everly. "Freedmen's Bureau Records: An Overview." *Prologue: Quarterly of the National Archives and Records Administration* (Summer 1997): 95–99.

Herbert G. Gutman. *The Black Family in Slavery and Freedom, 1750–1925*. New York: Vintage Books, 1976.

Records of the Freedman's Savings and Trust Company

Robert S. Davis, Jr. "Documentation for Afro-American Families: Records of the Freedman's Savings and Trust Company." *National Genealogical Society Quarterly*, vol. 76:2 (June 1988), pp. 139–146.

Carl R. Osthaus. *Freedmen, Philanthropy, and Fraud: A History of the Freedman's Savings Bank*. Illinois: University of Illinois Press, 1976.

Reginald Washington. "The Freedman's Savings and Trust Company and African American Genealogical Research." *Prologue: Quarterly of the National Archives and Records Administration* (Summer 1997): 170–181.

Records of the Commissioners of Claims

Frank W. Klingberg. *Southern Claims Commission*. California: University of California Press, 1955.

Philip D. Morgan. "The Ownership of Property by Slaves in the Mid-Nineteenth-Century Low Country." *Journal of Southern History*. August 1993, 49(3): pp. 399–420.

Reginald Washington. "The Southern Claims Commission: A Source for African-American Roots." *Prologue: Quarterly of the National Archives and Records Administration* (Winter 1995): 374–382.

Notes

"Country People" by T. Ramos Blanco.

Made in the USA
Middletown, DE
23 February 2016